A Bone in the Throat

Jane Taylor McDonnell

A Bone in the Throat

BLACK
WILLOW
PRESS

ISBN 978-0-939394-17-3

Published in the United States by Black Willow Press.
www.blackwillowpress.com

Book design by Mark F. Heiman
Cover and interior photos by Jane Taylor McDonnell

CONTENTS

ADAM AND EVE AT THE GATE

The angel stumbles a little in her new shoes
Not quite getting the straps right
In the shifting sands.
It's early and they didn't give her time
To get her make-up on.

She wonders why they asked her to sub on this one.
It looks like a job for Cherubim,
With flaming swords
To turn every which way.
In her hands she holds a hastily googled map
Of the Land of Nod. But this place before her —
Who could even call it a place —?
Not even a rock or bone would grow.

Then she sees them at the gate:
Damp and creased
Like children awakened
From too long an afternoon nap.
They lean into each other,
Taking shallow breaths.
They try to be brave the best they know how.

Her own light slices through them like chrome.
And then pity, a rock in her chest,
A bone in their throats.

SARAH LAUGHED

Why is it that all those inestimable women
Of the Old Testament
Must wait inside the tent?
Sarah may take pats of camel dung
Dried against the stone of the wall.
She stacks them with kindling
And strikes the flint.
She takes three measures of fine meal
And kneads and kneads.
She might then bake cakes upon the hearth.
But is told to wait inside the tent

Angels talk to men
And to other angels.
But it is always the woman who hears,
Who overhears, who ponders in her heart,
Who laughs with wonder,
With sorrow and delight,
Who knows.

THE ANGEL GABRIEL

And the angel Gabriel
Comes ratcheting down from heaven,
Catching his wings on the fig trees,
To have a word with Mary,
Who has found much favor with the Lord,
For washing Joseph's clothes
And wearing blue each Monday.

The torn wings hurt —
Their fine powder has come off
In his precipitous flight —
So Mary makes him chicken soup
And dresses his wings carefully.

He is very beautiful, dangerously so,
In his gold lame and silver chiffon wings.
And sweet too.
He seems to know all about her insides,
Things she doesn't dare mention to Joseph,
Things she scarcely understands herself.

When he gets up to leave, sweeping
His wings from the floor
And hunching his shoulders
To settle them back in place,
She feels a pang of sorrow.

"To have come this close, this close…"
She tells her Book Group later,
"…to something marvelous…"
She shakes her head
And picks up another Christmas cookie
Slowly licking the powdered sugar off her hand.

JEPHTHAH'S DAUGHTER

On clear days you can just make out
Jephthah's daughter, ascending
And descending the blue mountains:

She who was first forth from her father's house,
She who came out to meet him
With timbrels and with dance,
Her shy beauty just fledged.
Love shining in her gray eyes.

Oh, why could it not have been the hounds,
He thinks, who caught the first whiff of him
Home from doing bloody battle
With the Ammonites?
Why not the old servant, bent double
As he swept the courtyard
With his twig broom,
Or the black ram or the young kid
Caught in the thorn tree?

Why this only-born adored daughter
Who must now be given up
For a burnt offering?

And she begged of him just two months
Upon the mountains, that she might ascend
And descend taking her friends by her side,
That she might bewail her virginity.

So even now on a very clear day
You might see Jephthah's daughter
On the cold mountain slopes,
Moving among the thickets,
Releasing the dam,
The new-born kid,
From thorns in their sides,
And sending them — with a whack on the rump —
Down the mountain side and home again.

IPHIGENIA

It was never supposed to happen this way:
The daughter traded in for fair winds
And favorable tides,
The handsome ships outfitted for death
And seas as oily as any seduction.

She was supposed to be something quiet and apart
Wearing blue and thongs on her feet
And perhaps little wings when she needed them;
Not a bargain made on greasy papers by furtive fathers
In some back room of the gods.

She should have been able to slip
Into the purple shadows of a Greek afternoon,
With a book and a basket of plums,
To stand between earth and sky,
Not a blood sacrifice that begets another
And another and another,
Until all that is left are the furies,
Those bat-winged, leather pouches of fetid air.

I bring you back, Iphigenia,
In my daughter, in all our daughters:
The lovely bones of you
Standing at the edge of the sea,
The foam just curling over your sweet toes,
The wind died down, the tide always out.

FOR THE UNKNOWN DEAD

Story Overheard in a Writing Seminar

And the daughter was carried off
Kneeling and roped to the sides of the cart
Her wild voice hymn-singing
All the way to the gallows.

And the mother who sent her daughter
To the priest to be shriven of her sins
Sank to the frozen mud of the cow yard.
Beside her the priest
Who summoned the officers.

And before that the baby
Pitch-forked in the face
As soon as he was born
Steaming into the hay.

And before that the young soldier
Come to mend the barn
And geld the calves, who found
The daughter with her flaxen hair
Hanging like a rope to her waist,
And the straw already spun into gold
Beneath her.

       *   *   *

Did such things happen
In the old days with the cramp of hunger,
When even the heart seized up
And the lights went out
Over all the known world?

TO CALL IT INDIAN SUMMER

For Paul Thomas, b. August 6. 1970, d. August 6, 1970

When you come back to me it is always the dead end of the year,
The Doldrums, the Horse Latitudes.
To call it Indian Summer would be too kind.

They threw horses over the sides of ships
At this time of year, at the dead latitudes.
Caught in the slow spin of currents,
Of tides that never arrive,
No winds, the ships heaving and creaking
In nothingness.
No food for the horses, little for the men,
Caught in a rip tide that never ends,
A pause in earth-spin.

I grieve for you who never were,
The plain idea of you
The space you would have taken.

THE STONE, THE EARTH,
THE RAIN-SOAKED COLUMBINE

For Aisling, d. July 19, 2003

All day I have tried to make a story of your death,
Aisling, beautiful woman, dream vision,
Something deep and beautiful and necessary,
Not the death by car accident, a stupid blunder
Made by your boyfriend.

But there is only this hollow sound
As we walk the road from church to grave.

In a neighbor's garden stands a huge white lily,
Almost callous in its beauty.
A child's swing moves in the almost still air.
And then again: that peculiar silence
Made by hundreds of heels
Striking pavement over and over again.

Suddenly I feel them walking beside us:
The not-sound of naked feet bundled in rags,
The silenced whine of children,
The stopped up throat of the baby,
Still carried, the dead weight of him,
Walking beside us:
The famine dead.

There must be hundreds and hundreds of them,
Moving in from all over Ireland
Across the hungry grass.
Sometimes they touch us lightly —
You might mistake it for the wind —
A soft brush of fingertips
Across a cheek,
Stroking a hair back in place.

A whisper in a child's ear,
Your young brother's.
A hand beneath your mother's elbow,
Helping her to take another step
And another and another.

As they walk, they pick up the winds,
Warm gulf winds spun off the cold Atlantic.
They gather the birds — chaffinch and house wren —
Small hedge-dwellers to move just ahead of us.

And at your graveside:
Thousands and thousands of rose petals:
They have arranged to have them shipped in
So you, Aisling, might be lowered softly
Onto a bed of roses — red and fuchsia, pale pink,
Coral and magenta, peach and gold.

Then satisfied, they step back against the wall,
Hands clasped, eyes looking down.
"Sorry for your trouble."
"Sorry for your trouble."
And disappear once more into the stone,
The earth and the rain-soaked columbine.

FOR SHARON GATES-HULL

Died at intersection of MN Cty Road 9 and US 52

This is just to remind you there is a place
Off the highway to Rochester, MN,
A place where spring bounds in
And the wind is there to lift your soul
Into a little freshet of silence.

There you will find Indian Ponies,
Whose eyes will darken with kindness,
And the eternal silence
That will always love you as well.

And the happiness that ripples
The sides of the ponies will be yours
And if you wish you can break into blossom
And dance as you have always danced,
Spinning with the children
Who will take you with your long bones
And dance with them in paradise.

(with thanks to James Wright)

FOUNDLING

I was left on a cold hillside —
Exposed was what they called it —
Until found by poor shepherds
And raised as their own.
I returned to become my own terrible fate.

I was sent smiling and babbling
In a rush-woven boat-cradle down the Nile.
I was found by the daughter of the Pharaoh
Who raised me as her own, only to lose me
When I led my people out of bondage.

I was carefully placed in a double-door
On a threshold at Coram's Fields.
Found wrapped in my mother's despair,
I was taken in to die of smallpox.
No one knew my name.
Handel wrote my Anthem.

I was placed at the door of a theater
Because my mother had always heard
Players are kind. They named me
Catherine Variety Sheridan.

I was laid in a cradle at night
But found gone in the morning;
A fairy child was found in my stead.
They killed me with fire and iron and salt.
I died a terrible death.

I was left in a revolving foundling drawer,
Warmed and quickly found
By kind but judgmental nurses.
My mother was never found.
Nor did she want to be.

I was a carried in a woven basket
At Obama's first Inauguration, a basket
Made of sea-grass by my grandmother.
They named me India Arianna Grosvenor,
Child of Georgia Geechees, child of slaves.

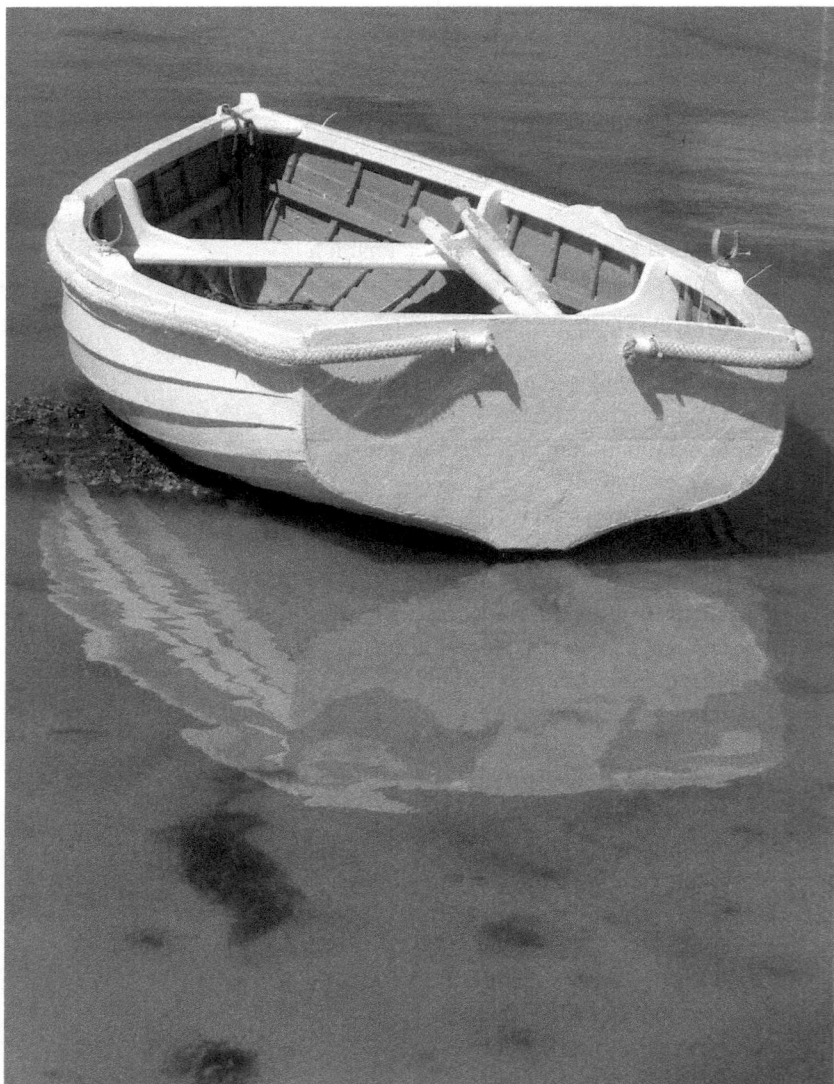

YOU ARE MADE OF

For Anthony

You are made of
The bones of elk,
The sink of bog,
And a tiny beaten golden boat.

You are made of the buttery lips
Of a Connemara pony,
Of sleeve nibbling goats
At a fence post,
Of St. Kevin's nesting hand.

You are made of long boats
And hacked off hands,
Of a fight on the edge of a field,
A fall on rocks, of a death
That lasted generations.

You are made of yellow haired
Summer soldiers,
Of women whose proud beauty
Would twist the heart
Right out of its socket.

BOGS ARE THE LAND LOSING ITSELF

There was little to warn us:
A few carnivorous plants,
Tender wet pitchers
Lifted to the low wind,
But no sucking at the feet,
No crazy glue at the ankles,
The shins, black paste
Creeping thigh wards.

We stood on little hillocks,
The safety of brown,
Crested mounds of grass and reed,
Stared into a green fluorescence,
A child's plastic glow-in-the-dark green.

The black hole
Just beyond
Meant nothing.

Until
Standing where I was
Gravity began to feel stronger,
As if the earth loved me
More than I wished to know.

Bogs, I once thought, are ancient:
Trees melted down to earth,
A whole tropical forest
Mashed into apple butter.
A dump site
Of all those generations past.

But bogs are new,
And happening right now.

Bogs are the land losing itself,
Pastures gone for grazing,
Trees gone for cutting and building
And burning. Acid leeching into the salmon falls,
Closing in on the sea.

They cut bogs of course,
The neat slices from the slane
Looking like wet shiny teeth.
Later we will take the heat from them.

But still the past is everywhere below.
It seeps into the tongues of our shoes.

THIS IS ONE WAY TO MAKE THE PAST

A monk sits in a cell.
Outside the window
It is Ireland
And it is raining.
Small needles of icy water stitch the ground.
They would be runneling down the gutters,
But the century is too early
And gutters haven't been invented yet.

Or maybe it is spring
Outside the window slit:
So green the eyes would smart,
Swallows rolling the air,
Sounds of the earth opening, the wind a blessing.

Inside you would probably see
A small rush bottom chair.
On it sits a monk.
Before him a slanted desk
Or table,
Made of bog oak
Or perhaps made of ash.

Lined vellum lies before him,
Small ink pots of Lapis Lazuli,
Azurite, Cadmium Yellow,
Arsenic and lead
Carefully concealed
In earth colors, sky colors.

He dips his fox tail brush
Into the Lapis,
Touches his tongue,
Pauses, thinks,
Watches his cat stand,
Stretch, wreathe,
Then coil close to the pots again.

Brush to tongue to pot to paper,
Laced serpents glow buttery yellow
And Mary's dress is bluer
Than all the packed leaves of heaven.

Angels, riding above all night,
Drag a golden net, but are gone by morning.

A SMALL PLACE, A SMALL TIME

I went down to the strand
And walked and ran in the wind.
It was your wedding day
And two horses and two riders
Came cantering
On the packed sand
As the tide was going out,
As the day was going out.
And one horse pranced sideways
Almost crabwise but high-stepping
And beautiful — delicate hooves
Lifted above the foam.

Afraid or feeling at home
By the sea, I could not tell,
As I did not know of myself
At that place land meets
Unfathomed sea,
The unknown forever pulling
At my feet,
Then releasing,
Pulling and releasing.

And I want to tell you
I was given that moment
As the two of you were given
Each other. I do not need to tell you
To treasure your small place
On the sand, between the sea and the land,
The small time between tide coming in
And tide going out, you the horse rider
And you the runner, to treasure your lives
With your life.

A GREAT SORROW

Was put upon my mother
That never she would tell.

Bottles and glasses
Behind doors, under sinks,
Rattled with her grief.

A hand once steady to paint
Wrung the rag from the pail
And covered the windows
Against the singing of the sun.

A dog's bowl, empty,
And nosed across the floor
Woke her from trance,
But not once could I cheer her.

She pinned herself to the line
And rode with the wind.
She dug herself under
With peat moss and mulch.

Sad in her single way
She stepped into her shadow
And stayed there.

In the end we laid her out:
A simple sad ceremony
Across her ironing board.

YOU, MY MOTHER

Were born on a cold night, into a gray dawn,
The fire banked too high and the chimney ablaze.
They say the men ripped floor boards back
Beside the bed, hacking in
To catch the fire,
Before the whole house went up.

Outside was dense with snow fog,
The doctor lost, the midwife at another birth,
The whole county shrouded in bitter ice.

Some bad fairy — disinvited —
Insinuated itself onto the hearth,
Rolled the coals on the rug,
Hissed the sparks onto sheet and quilt
And sat there, spitting out its venom.

It must have seemed that you, my mother,
Might have been caught forever
In your own mother, and she might have been
Caught in her own caul of death,

Until finally, finally,
Someone thought to answer the riddle,
To tell the spell backwards,
And you both were released.

Bone slipped from under bone,
The baby took up the cry,
The house was saved,
And the mother wept
Her own new born tears.

And all that is left of that night
Is burnt into the hearth:
The shape of a small baby curled on its side.

LISTEN

The time of your burial
Was an ice storm.
We arrived the night before
In dark cold, thinking
The energy grid for the whole world
Had sagged and snapped off.

The bank, the gas station,
The strip mall with its Chinese take-away:
Everything was hunched down in stunned silence.

The parking lot was full of ice pods
Peeled from twigs and split open down the back
Like the shells of cicadas.
You would have loved the way
They crunched under our feet.

A single blue bug light
Stood on the motel desk,
And our way upstairs
Was lit by a flashlight.

They left us with a snap-open glow worm,
The kind children use for Halloween:
All night its dull glow
Rubbed open a small place
In the darkness.

In the morning, under a burning sun,
The whole roof cap of ice slid off.
You would have loved the way
The world cracked open again
And the sun clapped its hands for joy.

A wonderful story to tell up there.

ANNUNCIATION

For Anthony

This is your first showing forth,
Little fingerling, little tear drop,
Little thumb of clay.
Only sound can see you:
Smoke in your mother.
Little tadpole, little newt,
Little shadow of a hawk's wing passing.

Little root,
Little snap bean,
Little pop of light:
We love you already
Before you are here to love.

Little burp, little bump,
Little pocket of cells.
You are a blue print of yourself.

I try bringing you lilies
On a shaft of light,
But I am no Gabriel.
Only a grandmother,
I cannot announce your place
Among the stars.

BY THE WATERS OF BABYLON

The grown man sat at the kitchen table and wept
Not allowed one day off after thirty years of work
Weeping at the kitchen table
The greens burned down to gray
On the back of the stove
Not allowed one day after thirty years
One day for the Graduation of his son
The rice boiling over the sides of the pot
Weeping at the kitchen table and not one day
The man my grandfather sat and wept after thirty years
Working for his cousin not given one day
The family standing mute
No meat for this day fatback for the collards
Boiling down not one day
As the Carolina sun dips in the west
Over the mountains Pickens
And Table Rock and Traveler's Rest
One day to see the graduation of his son
Weeping at the kitchen table a grown man.

By the waters of Babylon
He sat down and wept

THE END OF SUMMER

I

No time to sit on the yellow porch
In the black rocking chair,
To watch the Honey Locust tree
Dry in the wind,
To watch for the humming birds
Returned from Venezuela
Or to get down low in the grass
By the water and watch with the eye of a child
The Devil's Darning Needles go in
And out of some button hole of the air.
Or to see the yellow butterflies
Pitch their tiny tents on the cow dung,
Or slowly, slowly watch the Devil's Shoe Lace
Bind the pastures each to each.
No time to be a child again.

II

The car's headlights rake the side of the road
And the sticky white webs
Spun across the barbed wire.
"What is it?" you ask.
This is Manna. It means 'what is it?'
Be careful and taste it slowly.
It has come from heaven.

III

Luggage is still lost or stolen or left behind.
Locust trees are dying.
Rocks are covered with rust.
Now the hummingbirds start to leave for Venezuela
And my mother's dollhouse has entered its final decay.

Our grandfathers have long since flown into flinders,
The last finger cells gone from the house,
From the pages of accounting books,
From the Confederate money
In the final drawer of the final desk.
But look:
There sits my grandson on a stone
His two year old spine stiffened,
His look as proud as you please.

A RING LASTS LONGER THAN A FINGER BONE

At night I try to keep the outside out
And the inside in.
                    But still
I hear the soft sound of the Indian bones shuffling
Themselves together and tap
Tap, tapping on the window.

They have sent my granddaughter —
The one with the flaming red hair —
To sleep across the hall in the Yellow Room.

                    We read most
Of the night and I bless her
For not telling on me. This house
Is my refuge and my strength
Even with the ghosts whispering
Their sad confabulations
In the corner by the chiffarobe
Where I keep the funeral rings
And woven hair booches.

I know a ring lasts
Longer than a finger bone,
But it is the bones that rise up
And try to speak.

The dead slaves are sunk in their unmarked graves
Behind the apple orchard.
Their place has become a sinkhole.
Farmers throw their drums of Round Up
And broken tractors there.

This desecration goes unremarked
By all the family, but some day they will come for me — slaves,
Indians, great grandparents, the family dead of typhus —
And they will take me from this place
Which has known me in all my kind intentions and failings.

The mountains are purple like a bruise.
They do not bring me strength
I can no longer hear the sound
Of the ancient earth in wind or water.

At night I sleep with my dolls beside me.
Their faces are ruined, but once they seemed human.

THESE STORIES

Every Southern family has them.
The Bible snatched up by the maiden daughter
As she is carried away by Indians.
She returns with a baby
And generations later
I wonder about my mother's cheekbones.

The freed slave gone over to the Northern Army,
Annanaius returning home with rags on his feet
And gratitude in his rheumy eyes.
A sop of brandy each night, master and slave,
Until the day he dies.

The Letter of Forgiveness
To the Southern traitor of the Union
And of course the buried silver:
Isn't it always under leaves and a wheelbarrow
By cow pats in the barnyard?

The rope sent for John Brown's hanging:
Every family sent one
And boasted theirs was the thickest.
The scalp of the Indian sent home by the dying husband
To his ravaged wife.
The dead Union soldier — fourteen years old —
Buried out back beneath the live oak.
A letter is sent to his family in Boston.

Distillery boards beaten into church pews.
The last jeroboam of the most precious whiskey
Kicked over by our grandmother in the spring house.

The slave graveyard on the edge of the plantation
The Indian bones that come tapping at twilight.
The formal visit from the friend just dead.

One plantation house inhabited by goats.
Yet another sold to Northern Aggressors.
The toys hidden beneath the floor boards
So the child thinks he can return, although he never does.

The pack rats' nest found in the wall
Three generations later, with its kid glove,
Accounting papers and Belgium lace handkerchief.

Every white Southern family of a certain class…

FIRST JOB

My father's first job as a cub reporter in Columbia, SC, was to witness an electrocution, a death by electric chair. Doubtless the man was black; my father was white. I imagine them earlier, riding the rails together in temporary boxcar equality. I know my father rode the rails, but he had somewhere to go and a job whose purpose was (nevertheless) terrible.

Cub Reporter and nothing but words
And they all wrong,
All wrong, all wrong.
Electric chair, burnt air
All wrong.
Warden vomits into bag,
All wrong.
Retching, catching
The smell of burnt hair
All wrong, all wrong.
Boxcar was better.
No fare and riding the rails
With sparks and witch grass
Set fire by rails.
Pity frizzes out with smell of burnt hair,
Leaping electric air,
So wrong so wrong
Witnessing the witless.
Stumbling back to report
All gone, all wrong.
Nothing to report
Just the smell of burnt hair
Not there, not there.

YOU, ALECK

I think of you, Aleck,
With the body of your young master,
My great grandmother's brother,
Brought home in a boxcar, Southern Express:
Chickamauga to Graniteville,
That long, late hot summer day.
Did they let you open the door of the boxcar,
Sit with your legs dangling,
To watch the fields of the only life you knew,
The sick smell of death behind you,
A bottle of Pennyroyal or Peppermint Oil
To hold at your nose,
And hot, so hot it seemed the rails would melt?
You who cooked for him,
Washed his linen, sewed on buttons,
Knelt to pray with him at the end of day.
All those long, late, hot summer days.
You who carried him to the tent at the edge of the field,
Snodgrass Hill, Chickamauga, September 20, 1863,
You who were old, watching your young master die slowly,
All that long, late, hot summer day,
His uniform sticky with blood,
Almost a son to you
Who carried him as a child, bathed him in a zinc tub,
Lifted him over fences, fed him gumbo and rice.
You, Aleck, who had no last name,
But loved with a love we no longer understand,
All those long, late, hot summer days,
When the world you knew was ending
And another had yet to begin
You, Aleck, who had no last name.

THE GRAND HADRON COLLIDER

For Frank

It has something to do with deep heat
And far cold, with super-cooling
And super-conducting. With magnets
And beams of pure original light,
And almost, almost…
The ultimate, improbable beginnings
Of everything: the spark
Struck from the anvil
Of the unmoved mover.

It has to do with protons
Slung around by magnets.
And focus, it has to do with focus,
The shifting of shapes and settling.
With beams crossing or colliding.
And helium — 170 tons of the stuff.
Enough to float the earth?

But somewhere, somehow,
Someone made the primal mistake,
Got the numbers wrong —
It is always in the numbers,
Isn't it? — and settled the magnet
Into the wrong place,
Or put the copper wires
Too close together,
Or forgot about gravity,
Or leaked a few ions.
Who knows?

And the collider stopped.
For a while at least.

But then they got it right.
Quarks suddenly made sense.
The Higg's particle granted one shy appearance,
Acting suspiciously like molasses,
The Standard Model clicked back in.
The universe acquired mass
And kept on going…

OTHERWISE AND ELSEWHERE

London, 7/7

It happens to other people
Elsewhere:
Around the corner
In the Underground
And the next square over.
Backpacks exploded.
Blood in the eyes.
The stumble to safety with no feet.
The paper mask fitted tight
To the burned face
At the top of the stairs.
A cell phone recording black smoke,
Or nothing at all.

Hotel stewards rush with blankets and water
Around the corner to the tube station.
Brit Rail assembles in one room,
Police take over another as "staging area."

But nothing happens here
Inside the Woburn Room
Of the Russell Hotel on Russell Square.

Everything is elsewhere and otherwise,
Far from this windowless mirrored hall.

Inside it is eerily silent.
The telephone lines are shut down,
The TV confiscated for our own good:
We must not frighten our French visitors.
Even rumors die like deflated balloons.

Outside at Tavistock square a bus is torn open,
Sides pealed back like a tin can,
The shadows of people blown apart
On the walls of a bank.

Liverpool Street Station,
Edgeware Road Station,

Russell Square and Aldgate,
Kings Cross and Moorgate:
All shut down.
Trains are terminated at Luton.

No one moves in or out
Or around London,
Except on foot.
Cars and buses are pulled over
And abandoned.
The pigeons have left Russell Square.

Finally let out to return
To our rooms,
We walk the marble staircase
Over and over again.
Each time I reach
The bottom of the stairs,
I touch the brass dragon,
Put my hand in its mouth,
To feel for its two front teeth.

LAST THINGS

I

On the plane to my father's death:
These passengers that I don't see
Except for one of them,
The one who combs out her long yellow hair,
So happy, so happy she is to escape
Her parents. And I want to tell her soon enough
You will be on this small plane
To your father, to your mother,
As it struggles,
Then lifts over the mountain rim
Into sun and the light is flung like a blindfold
Across your face.

II

And in the church
A sudden hush:
Rain on the high tin roof,
As if millions and millions
Of tiny hands
Reached for us.
Or as a mother's hand
Might rest soft
On the warm, beating fontanel
Of her baby's head.

III

Fourteen years later,
Your matches still wait in my cupboard:
One for each pipe you didn't light.
Slowly I use them
Each one a little Lucifer,
A flare of sulfur, quickened
Then dead.

Nothing is more final
Than a flame going out.
Except for one thing,
Except for one thing:
You, dear one, winking out.

WHAT THE GRANDMOTHER SAID

I am like earthworms on the street
After a rainstorm. I am
The dead end of winter when
The rabbit's house is breached
And the nestlings are left to die.

I am the one-legged crane
Patiently watching
The polluted pond.

My sorrow has no name.
No one will say it in a book of fates.

Above me the Haggard circles.
His prey will be tiny and bitter.

FOR KATE

Your voice on the phone:
It travels the seafloor and up to the stars.
A click, then a pause. "Mom!" you say,
As if startled to find me
In my own kitchen
Where I have been all along,
As you travel to Malaysia, to Thailand,
In Cambodia and India buying me a scarf:
A beautiful thing,
The color of sea and stars,
Of jungle fog and the long unraveled breaths
Of baby elephants, of spirit houses
And all the spirits they house,
Of Saffron monks and silver begging bowls,
Of sandals left at temple doors,
Of being lost and found again,
Lost and found again.

The string your voice weaves,
The answering thread of mine.

WISH

In my dream I won a house,
A whole, white painted brick house
With chimneys and beautiful
Small casement windows up near the eaves,
And always summer outside
And inside furniture and a life
Waiting to be lived,
A house for my son and daughter-in-law
And grandson because she had seen a picture
In a magazine and loved the Gothic (Late Perpendicular)
Windows (their odd way of being):
And I won it, the house, in a magazine contest,
Never dreaming in my dream
That I could win and my son saw comets
Through each of the windows
And I wanted them to be there and happy
And happy when I am gone.

IRON NIGHTS, COPPER DAYS

After Reading Beowulf

Hard cold.
The old gods walk our hills again, pace the shadow lines.
Iron nights, copper days — if we have any luck at all.
Our bone-lappings loosen, crack in the long dark,
Ache when we wake in querulous confusion.

Ground gods stir and upheave the frost-bitten hills,
Scum the sides of buffalo and the fence-jumping calf,
Shaggy in his grief, searching for his mother.

The wind moves in through Buffalo Gap
Then passes beyond.
We huddle together, family and dogs,
Each searching for rank and place by the fire,
Hoarding our kinship beneath the rafters,
Each a cousin to our cousins on the long benches.

Outside the sting of the wind
Seeks the crack in the boards.
Inside, our threshold holds in our hoardings,
Heaped treasures of long held stories,
Gold threads teased from the weavings
Of flax and sheep-shearings.

Soon enough the bone-house will be harrowed,
Our limbs unstrung from their moorings,
The fine finger bones loosened from sinew.
The fire will burn on the barrow,
Our bodies' hoardings ransacked by flames,
And the long tomorrows stretch out over the hills.

FIRE DANCER

You dance with the flames,
Advance against darkness,
Each finger dipped in kerosene
Flaring forth gold vermilion.

I watch from the dark fields
Beyond, trembling for you
Who will not shake, steady on
The rolling dark,
Level with the twilight air.

I suck in my breath.
I will not disturb you, but will hold the air
And release it into your pure being.

THE WITCH OF WINTER

Last week I saw her
Climb into her SUV,
Twitch her cloak aside
And slam the door.

She drove off, of course,
But not before I caught a glimpse
Of her purple pink hounds,
Docked tails thumping
On the flip down seat.

It was obvious they had swallowed
The year whole and were licking
Their chops, small smiles
Snickering around their black lips.

But what did she care,
With a full load of groceries,
A half cord of firewood,
Claret bottles clinking,
And the best traction in the world?

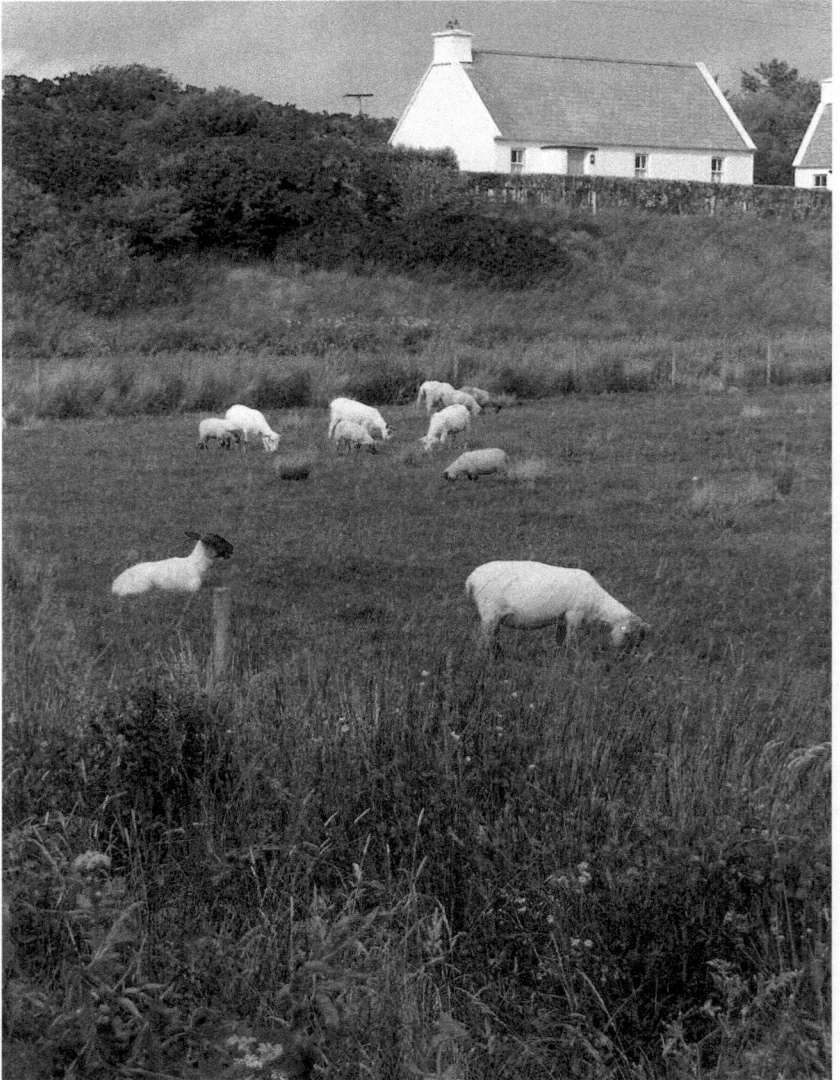

THIS YOUNG CALF

We pull over by the side of the road,
Speak to the farmer who says
He wishes he had a dime for every calf
He's seen born and so remains inside
His ammonia-smelling kitchen
And back stairs.

But we, my son and I,
Have never witnessed this particular mystery,
This wringing out of a white pulp that moves
In its slickery-skinned caul,
All knee-knobs and knick-knack paddy-wack
Give – the – dog – a – bone,
And this young calf — all stumble bumble —
Comes rolling home.

THE OWL EATS

The vole whole, bones and fur,
And teeth and all.
It eats the memory of small, neat things
At the end of the barrow,
Earthlinks of roots,
Seeds of grasses,
The definitions of dirt seen close up.
The owl eats thimbles of mouse milk,
The litter of bugs and babies left behind,
Earth's edgelings,
The tender limits of life
On a crust of snow.

CHAT

For Frank and Tony

The Chiffchaff chits at us from willows,
And the Willow Warbler wears a biker's helmet,
Snugged to his head and tipped back red.
The Ringed plover is indeed ringed,
Just as the Turnstone flips stones like hamburgers
With the Rock Pippet who also works
The rocks by the edge of the sea.

The Sanderling runs in and out
Of the surf —
That is easy enough to remember —
And the Common Coot has
Bloated digits for a good reason.

But who could have thought up
The bastard wing and the high lift
At low speeds of the cliff hanging,
Wind walking, rock shearing
Peregrine Falcon?

POEM FOR ENGLISH MAJORS

Of course the Rooks delight heaven,
Just as the heavens delight the Rooks,
Especially at evening as they circle
And circle and pull the drawstring tighter
And tighter on the velvet night.

They are beautiful and necessary
As they come in from the fields
To settle by the old church.

The day couldn't end without them.

But not everyone sees them this way,
And to keep them away the town fathers
Have lopped off the trees at the knees.

But I want to say:
How can you have forgotten so soon
The mackerel crowded, the wine dark seas,
The house martens and the air that smells
So wooingly there, the westrun wind,
The small rain, the valley of the shadow,
And the brightness that falls from the air?

Let alone Aprile with his shoures sote,
The busy old fool, unruly sun,
The green thought in a green shade,
The sick rose, the tigers of wrath,
A much of a which of a wind, and
The kind ponies by the road to Rochester, Minnesota?

LION HOUSE

The lion drew my father — that loose-limbed,
Foot dropping, hungry pace
Across the hosed down cement floor.

Oh, the wonder, the pride, the majesty, the elegance.

All of which I could see, but for six-year old me
It was the smell that filled my head,
That desperate, coffined stink
On a hot DC day.

Cats have no smell:
They lick and lick and lick.
But this stench would have carried
On any wind.

So when my father told me
The story of the two year old child,
Brought by her grandfather
To admire this wonder of the world,
Of how she (the child)
Reached through the bars of the cage
And of how he (the lion)
Simply reached out one paw
And hooked her little head,
Right through those bars,
I understood.

There are some things
We cannot hope to have
In this world.

GOLDBERG VARIATIONS

What would they be without Glenn Gould's
Humming narrative?

This speech of the Gods
Would simply float off to heaven
With us tethered by a thread, until
Too high in the stratosphere,
The stratospause, we — holding on
For dear life by the skin of our teeth —
Would have to drop back onto
This hard, cold, flat earth of ours.

THE WOLF

For my Father, d. Nov. 14, 1994

I come to see you for the last time
After the other last time.
You approach slowly.
The chain link fence rattles a little
In the bitter wind. The late November light
Pricks the tips of your fur.

I place my hand flat on the fence links
Letting you sniff and rub, sniff and lick.
Then I say those strange human words
Telling you of my sorrow.
And you lay your long muzzle
By my hand on the mesh.
You lean into me,
Your heavy body laid all along the fence.

Then you lift your head
For a long cry of pain.
You say what I cannot say.
You call on thousands of years
Of two creatures
Inhabiting the earth in the same way.

I had lost my voice in my grief
But you take it up, singing the long sorrow
Beyond words.

You lick my fingers and it feels
Like his old tired hand patting my hand:
That's enough now, sweetie,
That's enough, he said.
And you turn away now,
The dropping sun glinting
Off the tips of your fur
And go to your spot, circling once,
Circling twice, then sinking into it with a sigh.

And I thank you for turning the terrible
Into the almost matter of fact.

THE TENDERNESS OF EAGLES

All this bleak not yet spring
Only the eagles are constant,
Held in their half-ton nest
In the forked branches
Of a cottonwood tree.

First the eggs — three of them
Kept warm by the mother/father.
Eggs gently turned by a long yellow beak
The warm breast feathers
Fluffed and settled so carefully
Each side, then the beak reaching out
To draw in the straw and twigs.
More careful settling down.

Then the hatchlings.
It takes all day, twenty-four hours,
To break though
The pip of the shell.

Then the weaklings, gray soft feathers
Fluffing them. So frail,
They fall on their faces,
Raise their funny little wings
Backwards at the elbow.
Feet too large, yellow and stumbling.

Then the feedings — from the rabbit larder
On one side, the fish on the other,
Tiny open mouths lifted,
The parent beak turned sideways
To insert a piece of fish skin,
A tendon of rabbit.

And I think when things get too hard,
Or go too soft with me, they are still there
At the press on a few buttons
On my computer.
And I draw strength from them.

But I am waiting for the cruel, predatory eyes,
The still hanging in the wind,
The wide circle closing,
The noose drawing in.

BALLOON OVER CAPPADOCIA

We feel no wind, no movement,
Are one with the air. Beneath us
Hard volcanic ash as far as the eye can see:
The inside of the earth has pushed itself out
And is already wearing itself down.

Ishmael guides us, dances in the ropes,
Pulleys, flaps, propane gas tanks,
We flare and rise. Improbable clowns,
We become an exhalation of the earth.

Beneath us the Anatolian and Arabian plates
Grind against each other, planning the next terror.
Under the rocks the churches stay damp and deserted,
The monks with their fat, protein deficient bellies
Long since gone to bone. The lands, already dead,
Salted by Romans to make them even more dead.

But here in middle space we are clothed in air,
The wind is without wind, we skim
The brightening ground, all lily pink and purple
And pale hyacinth. I reach over the basket
To pick an herb and touch a bush
Never before touched, as it will never be again.

Wood pigeons nest in the deserted rocks,
At night the minarets light up emerald green.
When Neil Armstrong walked
That other moonscape, the people here
Left their caves. Too shamed
To be called Troglodytes
So late in human history.

INDIA

See this, remember this:
An old woman stooped in a sari,
Clipping wheat by hand, a child
By her side bending it
Into a tiny stook. A mud hut,
Dung stacked for drying.
No wind for winnowing,
Only a hand-cranked fan.
An old man squatting in a ditch
Near a holy site, scooping water
Up under his loin cloth. A cow
Stunned, snuffling up black garbage bags.
Children crouching in doorways
Not asleep, not awake,
Waiting for milk in pales
Scoured out by dung and sand.

II

Until five years ago the world
Was a rumor gone thin as smoke
Or an eagle pitting the sky, soon gone.
Your temple door is the size of a child's body
A very small child's body,
And the deep familiar smell
Is the cow downstairs
As you sleep in the straw upstairs
Shifting softly in your dreams.

And the tock tock you hear
Is your mother's loam outside
In the first light
Before the rice fields blaze up
In their unreal greens
And the monkeys come yet again
To eat the apple blossoms
As you try to slingshot them off.

The side of this mountain
Has always been slipping down into the valley,
Just as your grandfather gathers twigs
All summer and creeps down
Like a giant tortoise,
And your mother slaps your clothes
On the edge of the cistern
And snaps you back with her black eyes
From the last picture I just took
To show you to yourself
In your world.

POINT OF VIEW

When my aunts bought the place in the foothills
and being of literary bent named it
Point of View so we might have a place
from which to view the rains —
veils blowing across the coves and hollows
blue and white and hyacinth grey, and a point on a hill
where the tin roof rattled and the wood-fired stove
served up three kinds of beans — runner and snap and butter,
cornpone, greens and fatback, hominy and red-eye gravy,
hush puppies and tomatoes so fat and juicy
they slapped the plate on the way down
from the knife's edge. Beef-Steak tomatoes
we called them. And sleeping on the porch afterwards
was the best part, the rain still making
its smoky way across the valleys,
near Paris Mountain and Traveler's Rest.
And the smell of the rain and the fatback
and the wood and the kerosene under the eves
was the second best part
where the Mud Daubers had built their cities.
And did I mention the Piccalilli and pickled peaches
and Coblers and peaches with the fuzz still on
rubbing off on our chins so peach fuzz was the last thing
we tasted at night.

II

And when my aunts moved to Assisted Living
across the street from the Confederate Museum,
where the blood soaked jacket of their great uncle
in its glass display case
dried and cracked a little more each day,
and they never once walked over there to see it.
And why should they? And as they got smaller each day,
One hundred and two, one hundred and four,
the years were posted on banners
In the dining room (it was such good publicity),
and the TV crews were called out
only to be sent packing.

III

And why didn't I bring them the lightening bugs
in a Mason Jar, its top punched full of holes,
and let them out one by one
to fly and light and pulse against the ceiling,
to rest on the curtains, wings fanning, bellies throbbing,
so many of them, so many they would make a smoky haze
of mountain distance, of owls speaking to the moon,
of watermelon rinds eaten right down to the quick.

AFTER THE FIRST DARK

For Muna

After the boy soldiers have left,
After the first dark settled with the dust,
And the blood started to congeal,
And the flies left for the night,
And the sticky bloat set in,
When even the air was too stunned
To vibrate with outrage —
Then it was you ran out with you teenaged friends,
Out of the camp, out for a lark,
To pull the dead back in to the tents.

Then it was you found the live baby
On the dead mother's back,
Lifted him carefully,
Back to the life he would not have chosen,
As you would not have chosen this life
You now tell me of.

You sit back quietly in my office chair.
Behind us the sky is neatly squared off
In a Minnesota winter.
The snow could not look more innocent.

How old were you, is all I can think to ask,
Fourteen, you tell me. Much older
Than I am now.

                 And I think:
There are so many ways
To fail a child.

TEMPLE DUST

For Vaddey

There is a place in a Cambodian temple
Where, when you stand in a doorway,
Your heart beat, your chest drum, is magnified,
As if the stones themselves live
In their jacket of jungle.

We tourists try standing there,
One after another,
Each listening to the wonder
Of this ancient Electrocardiogram.
Sound magnifies as we beat on our chests.
A young man's beat is loud,
Mine much softer.

This is the place where the trees
Have strangled the stone,
Where at dusk pink lies on everything,
Like the fairy dust we carry back to our hotel rooms.
This is the place
Where the gold has been twisted from the Buddha's eyes,
Where the river reverses itself once each year
And flows backward,
Where monks wear the colors of stone
Only more so,
Where dancers in stone,
Restored and catalogued
By German professors,
Have been rubbed smooth on belly and breast.

A place unguarded,
Guarded, lost for centuries,
Found, lost again, found again,
Before some final loss.

But — to go back to our hearts
Beating in stone — mine was softer,
As I said. And closer to dust
Than yours, my dear.

INTERVIEWING THE GHOST

For Kate

You lived in a governor's mansion over the bay
And Charlotte Amalie where the ships came in.

Trees fought for those hills.
Pissarro painted their struggle.
Roosters told each hour through the night
And set off dogs on every hill.

It was beautiful, but ruined:
Those improbable tropics
Where fruit trees tasted of bubble gum
And iguanas crashed off the porch like tiny tanks.

For three years, you lived there. You adapted.
I remember the bright green flipper in the trunk of your car
Kept to coax baby iguanas from the trees.

You worked as teacher and tour guide
In a Lewis Carroll hat. Your office was a beach.
The sands were white and clean
But some trees rained poison.

When you stripped the plaster from the kitchen walls,
The ants came in for the molasses.
Molasses once held that world together.
Even now, all time there is Back Time.

A TV crew came to interview your ghost but you said
Only the cat Pandora padded in and out.
Later the white man ghost eased himself
Back in, smelling faintly of ashes.

When we visited we slept under mosquito netting,
Beautiful as cobwebs. Once your Rastafarian friend
Cooked me a mess of collard greens, as his neighbors hissed
"You not welcome here whitey."

I remember the wind blew off the sea in the morning,
Off the land at night. It was always cool there
And the rafters spoke of sun, of tides, of trades.

I miss you, my daughter, in that place, in that time.

A NEST OF CINNAMON

All nursing homes seem to have them:
A large cage full of birds,
Tiny sparks struck from the cruel flint of this world.

Dying might seem less difficult,
Or so the thought goes,
Beside this fling of seeds,
This pout of feathers,
The tiny heads gone under a wing,
The whole soul rocking off
Sweetly, mid-afternoon.

Perhaps that is the way I will go,
And it will seem not so bad.
They will simply sing me away
To join all the others,
Phoenix and Firebird,
Trumpeter Swan and common goose,
Owl's body nailed to the barn door,
The cuckoo calling from north, from south,
And the St. Stephen's Day wren
Buried in the churchyard
To await another spring.

I will fly to a high nest of frankincense
And cinnamon to sing the sun
On its way. And so will come another night,
Another day.
Another night.
Another day.

VARANASI

This is the river crossing,
The place for the final fording.
Here Shiva is said to whisper in your ear
The ferry boat song.
Here you might leave this life and all lives
With marigolds and candles to light your way.

It is meant to be easy:
Too late for sorrow to catch
Like a bone in your throat.
You must burn cleanly
With the holy kusha grass and the embers
Kept for a thousand years.

Here no woman can watch your passing
And pull you back with her tears.
You must not return out of pity.
Or love. Or revenge.

You must await your turn on the ghat,
The holy stairs, above the dank,
Slow-swinging river.
A small heap of silks on a litter.
Thin. Still.

Your son is here to break your skull.
After that it is supposed to be easy.

Do not see those other sad, damp rags cast aside.
Or the bone crushers and the beaters
And the dealers in death.

Forget that the spirit does not separate easily from its bone,
Fiber upon fiber remaining.

Forget the gold pickers, the silver thread pullers,
The harvest of ash and bone.

Forget the blasphemous blue boats
Where we watch from the river.

Forget that I have seen you
And be on your way.

POEM FOR THE FIRST DAY

Listen to me now: nothing is lost.
See how the water closes over the dropped stone
And heals itself. Not a pucker is left
On the still surface.

The rain falling today on a little town
In the west of Ireland
Came from the Caribbean a week ago
And not a drop of it was lost.

Right this moment an island
Is pushing itself up from the rim of the Pacific.
It will be named and called new,
But really it doesn't change a blessed thing.

By the Ganges, ashes lift on the wind
From the Burning Ghats,
Past indifferent monkeys
Climbing palace walls.
But even there, nothing is lost.

The meteorite just spun off
From the asteroid belt
Will be found on Tuesday in the Netherlands.
Or it will land by sheep
In a Patagonian pasture.
Or it might just vaporize
Over Cappadocia.
It does not matter where.

Listen to me now.
If you are very still
You will hear the earth
Turning on its axis,
The stars singing
In their clusters.

And all that is as it is.

Acknowledgments

Two poems, "Iphigenia" and "The Angel Gabriel" were first published in *Oberon Poetry*, Seventh Annual Issue, 2009.

Grateful acknowledgment is made to the members of Penchant, Northfield Women Poets, who read and made suggestions for many of these poems. Thanks to Mark Heiman for artistry in the production of this book, especially for the cover and for reproducing my photographs within the text. I would also like to thank most especially three other readers, Robert Tisdale, Keith Harrison and James McDonnell, the last of whom read and re-read and read yet again all of these poems.

www.ingramcontent.com/pod-product-compliance
Lightning Source LLC
Chambersburg PA
CBHW060036050426
42448CB00012B/3041